JOB Survival

Instructor's Manual

How to Adjust to the Workplace and Keep Your Job

Second Edition

by Dixie Lee Wright

Job Retention Specialist

JIST Works

America's Career Publisher

Job Survival Instructor's Manual
How to Adjust to the Workplace and Keep Your Job
Second Edition
© 2005 by Dixie Lee Wright

Published by JIST Works, an imprint of JIST Publishing, Inc.
8902 Otis Avenue
Indianapolis, IN 46216
Phone: 1-800-648-JIST   Fax: 1-800-JIST-FAX
E-mail: info@jist.com   Web site: www.jist.com

Note to instructors. This instructor's guide supports the student workbook entitled *Job Survival: How to Adjust to the Workplace and Keep Your Job,* Second Edition (ISBN 1-59357-120-8). The workbook and many other career-related books are available from JIST publishing.

Quantity discounts are available for JIST products. Please call 1-800-648-JIST or visit www.jist.com for a free catalog and more information.

Visit www.jist.com for information on JIST, free job search information, links to other career-related sites, book excerpts, and ordering information on our many products.

Visit CareerOINK.com for free information on 14,000 job titles.

Also by Dixie Lee Wright:
Job Survival: How to Adjust to the Workplace and Keep Your Job
Job Smarts: 12 Steps to Job Success
Job Smarts Instructor's Manual
Acquisitions Editor: Randy Haubner
Development Editor: Jill Mazurczyk
Cover and Interior: Aleata Howard
Proofreader: David Faust

Printed in Canada
08 07 06 05 04   9 8 7 6 5 4 3 2 1

ISBN 1-59357-121-6

About This Instructor's Manual

This manual was created to accompany the workbook titled *Job Survival: How to Adjust and Keep Your Job*. The workbook is designed to help anyone who had been out of the workplace for various reasons, has had trouble keeping a job, or has a situation that may affect job survival. The workbook may be especially helpful for individuals in the following groups: lower reading level, special needs, TANF, "at-risk" youth, school to work, and corrections. Many chapters in the workbook will require a person to examine their character and ethics and their ability to stay on a job by choice.

While the workbook is written in simple, direct language, this instructor's manual will help you clarify important points, stress critical job retention issues, and lead students through the material as desired.

Each workbook chapter has a corresponding chapter in this guide. You will find the following helpful, timesaving material in each chapter:

- Chapter objectives

- Rationale for this topic

- Working vocabulary

- For discussion

- Presentation suggestions

- Group and individual activities

Together with the workbook's examples, worksheets, questions, and checklists, this material will help your students learn how to handle the challenges of keeping their jobs.

Special Acknowledgment

My special thanks to my husband Lendon for his encouragement and his endless hours on the computer in putting this book together. His review, comments, and input were of great value. I could not have done it without him.

Additional Acknowledgments

I would like to thank the following people who endorsed this edition:

Tish Tyler
District Work-Study Coordinator
Albuquerque Public Schools

Priscilla L. Bohl
Employer Services Division
Mayor's Office of Workforce Development
Denver, CO

Butch Dalhaus
Education for Employment #330
Tech Prep Coordinator
Rantoul, IL

Sylvia Stoner, CRC
Counselor, Vocational Rehabilitation Services
Division of Disability, Aging & Rehabilitative Services
Indianapolis, IN

Jan Edwards
Job Placement Specialist
Owner of the Employment Connection
Denver, CO

Contents

Introduction

Suggestions for the Instructor

Provide each student with a bright yellow folder on the first day of class. This will be used to compile important lists and motivational materials. As the instructor, you may choose to have students include more or fewer items in their folders than mentioned in this guide.

Small group rotation is key. Assign each student a number, and then create groups based on even, odd, multiples of, and so on. Be creative, but try not to allow the same groups to form at every class meeting. Part of the course is learning to get along with many different kinds of people.

"Until Next Time" activities are preview sections that ask the students to think about an idea, concept, or action as it pertains to them. These are provided in lieu of specific homework assignments. Students may write answers if you prefer.

Some in-class exercises require written responses and the use of descriptive words. Compile a list of "outlaw words" or "stop words" that students may not use. Post these in a prominent spot where they may be easily seen by the entire class. Include on the list types of words, such as derogatory terms and curse words, as well as words like "good," "nice," "fun," "easy," and so on, because these say little about how a student actually feels or thinks.

An optional introductory activity follows. If time allows, the activity will help to focus the class on the subject at hand as well as act as an icebreaker.

Introductory Activity

The Good, the Bad, and the Future

Objectives: Set the tone for the coursework, provide a focal point for the students, encourage thought about past and future job experiences

Format: Individual to whole group

Time: 20–30 minutes

Materials: 3-by-5 index cards, pens, chart paper, marker

1. Write the following statements on the board or overhead while reading them aloud to the class:

   The best job I ever had was _____

   My boss was effective because _____

   I worked well there because I was able to_____

   _____

2. Pass an index card to each student. On the blank side of the card, ask students to write the word "BEST." On the lined side, have them write one or two words to fill in each blank in the statements. Then direct students to set aside their cards.

3. Write the following statements on the board or overhead while reading them aloud to the class:

   The worst job I ever had was _____

   My boss was not effective because _____

   I did not work well there because I was able/not able to _____

4. Pass a second index card to each student. Ask students to write the word "WORST" on the blank side of the card. On the lined side, have them write one or two words to fill in each blank and set aside.

5. Write the following statements on the board while reading each aloud:

   A job I think I will have in the future is _____

   I will look for a supervisor who is able to _____

   I will work well in this position because I will _____

6. Pass a third index card to each student. On the blank side of the card, ask the students to draw a question mark. On the lined side, have them fill in the blank for each statement with one or two words and set aside.

7. Ask random volunteers to read aloud their "?" card responses.

8. Place a chart paper titled "?" on the board or a wall. Allow at least two more students to read their responses. Then pause and ask, "Are any of their responses similar in any way?"

9. Write the similarities on the "?" chart paper.

10. Call on each student randomly until every student has read the "?" responses aloud. Instruct students to raise their hands every time they hear the similarities listed on the chart paper.

11. Continue in the same way for the "WORST" and "BEST" responses.

12. When all three charts are displayed, look for similarities on the "BEST" and "?" charts. Make a ceremony of throwing away their worst experiences.

13. Keep the two charts posted in the classroom for potential motivation. They may be read at the beginning of each session as an attention getter.

Chapter 1

Objectives

- Understanding that the workplace is always changing—and that you must adjust to it.

- Dealing with personal needs and barriers.

- Preparing for labeling and complaints.

- Deciding what type of worker you want to be.

Your Wake-Up Call

Rationale for This Topic

This is your SURVIVAL WAKE-UP CALL.

The work world is changing rapidly.

You need to see the work site as it is, not as you would like it to be.

You must adjust to the work site. The work site will not adjust to you.

To survive a job in the real world, here is REAL STUFF YOU NEED TO KNOW.

Working Vocabulary

- **Effect.** An effect is the result of an action.

- **Barrier.** A barrier is anything that stops you from doing something or going somewhere.

- **Multicultural.** A multicultural setting combines many different ideas, people, backgrounds, behaviors, and customs.

For Discussion

Now more than ever, due to the shrinking job market, it is important that you are able to survive on your job by choice. The words "wake up" immediately alert you to the fact that the workplace contains surprises. Most of these surprises can be eliminated if you recognize the real workplace as it is, not as you want it to be. You need to wake up.

If you are new to the workplace or have not been in the workplace for long, you are not prepared for the unexpected stuff you have to deal with. You are concerned only about your job duties. You are not prepared for the changing workplace environment, the complaints and labeling by co-workers, and how your different needs affect your ability to keep the job.

Everyone has concerns in the workplace. But not everyone has an added need or barrier to overcome in the workplace. It does not matter where you are coming from. If you are taking a first job, returning to work after a long absence, or are having trouble keeping a job, then you have a different job need than the average worker.

People who have not worked for some time or who have different needs do not lose their jobs because they cannot do the job. They lose jobs because they cannot adjust to the working environment.

Wake up! You are being challenged. You are being challenged to prove you can do the job. Can you accept the challenge? Or do you think you should not have to prove yourself? Remember: You must fit into the workplace. The workplace will not fit around you.

Presentation Suggestions

Use with Pages 2–4

As you begin the course, direct attention to the chapter objectives. Explain that the objectives will be presented prior to each class session. Present the Chapter 1 objectives and then ask the students to come up with one word that links all the objectives together. (Answer: change.) Write it on the board or overhead.

Introduce the working vocabulary and discuss the definitions. Present these prior to the beginning of each chapter. Be brief. Although the students may be familiar with some of the vocabulary, it is important to review.

Using the list on workbook page 2, have the students read around the room. Each student should read one word, describing the effect of the change and the emotions that accompanied the change.

Example: Dress code. **Effect:** People in many companies can dress less formally for work. **Emotion:** People can feel more comfortable at work and are happy about not buying as many dressier clothes.

After completing this exercise, have students complete the Stop and Think exercises on pages 2–4.

Use with Pages 13–17

Print the words "LISTEN" and "BREATHE" in bold letters on the board. Print the word "COMPLAINT" above it. Invite a student to read the three paragraphs under "You Must Deal with Complaints About You" on pages 13–14 aloud. Every time the word "complaint" is read, direct the students to pause and repeat the words "listen, breathe." When the reading is complete, ask the students, "Why did you repeat those words over and over? Can you think of when those words may help you in a future work situation?" Then, have students complete the Stop and Think on page 14.

Invite a student volunteer to read aloud the two paragraphs on pages 14–15 under "Understand Your Feelings About Co-workers." Then have students complete the Stop and Think on pages 15–16.

Using the list of labels on pages 15–16, ask each student to choose four words that describe someone with whom they work. Explain that these words must also describe the type of worker they would like to be. If you have not yet done so, pass out a yellow folder to each student. Ask students to write the four words they chose neatly on the outside of the folder. Remind the class of the following point: *If you practice the behaviors that you want from co-workers, chances are good that they will also behave that way. Be the model— demonstrate good workplace behavior yourself!*

Ask students to complete the Stop and Think on pages 16–17 in small groups. Explain that they should be able to use some words that they wrote on their folders.

Until Next Time

Have you ever heard the saying, "All my ducks are in a row"? That statement has to do with something called **priorities**. All people have a set of priorities. Some people's priorities never change while others' priorities change from day to day. There is a happy medium between those two. Before the next class, think about your life. Are all your ducks in a row, or are some of them having trouble staying afloat?

Activities

Ch-Ch Change

Use: After students complete the Stop and Think exercises on pages 2–4

Format: Small group to whole group

Time: 15 minutes

Materials: Markers, index cards

1. After students complete pages 2–4, explain that they will be exploring the idea of change in their own lives in more depth.

2. Break the class into small groups of three to four students.

3. Give each group two index cards with the following questions:

   • When have you felt good about a change? What was the change? Why was it good?

   • When has a change made you feel badly? What was the change? Why was it difficult?

4. Allow 8–10 minutes for each group to discuss responses among its own members.

5. Ask for a volunteer from each group to provide a brief review of what the group discussed. Suggest that the volunteer share some of each group member's responses.

Not So Soup-er Labels

Use: With pages 10–12

Format: Small group to whole group

Time: 20–25 minutes

Materials: 10 soup-can labels or copies of soup-can labels, markers, pens, paper, workbook pages 10–12

1. Break the class into small groups of three to four students.

2. Show one of the labels and ask the students to guess the topic of the next activity. (Answer: labeling.)

3. Pass out one soup-can label to each group. Each label should bear a different statement from page 11.

4. Explain to the groups that they will be responsible for role-playing a workplace situation where the statement is used and the labeled worker reacts. These skits should be no more than two or three minutes long. The role-play should show two worker reactions (appropriate and inappropriate).

5. Have students perform the skits for the whole group. Ask students to identify the appropriate reactions and how they differ from the inappropriate reactions. Discuss why appropriate reactions are a better choice.

6. It is important to bring to the attention of students that many people label things every day without recognizing it as labeling.

7. Go around the room one at a time. Read a label and have the student give one word that describes this person.

Policeman	Native American	Nun
Wrestler	Homeless person	Fireman
Pilot	Teacher	Mexican

Lawyer	Male ballet dancer	Gang member
Soldier	Arab	Teacher's pet
Bossy child	Stripper	Circus performer
Car salesman	Artist	Japanese person
Hooker	Doctor	Ugly girl
Governor	Pro football player	Boy with thick glasses
Principal	Saleswoman	Hockey player
Dentist	Preacher	
Skateboarder	Straight "A" student	Girl basketball player

8. Have an open discussion about the words the student chose to associate with the different labels.

Chapter 2

Objectives

- Learning different ways to prioritize.

- Seeing how values and principles affect priorities.

- Considering other issues that affect priorities.

- Knowing that your priorities will change.

Prioritizing

Rationale for This Topic

This is your SURVIVAL POWER.

The practice of prioritizing can mean success or failure in most paths you will take.

Prioritizing forces you to focus on first things first.

This is REAL STUFF YOU NEED TO FOCUS ON.

Working Vocabulary

- **Priority.** A priority is anything you believe is more important than other things.

- **Principle.** A principle is a standard or quality considered worthwhile or desirable.

- **Value.** A value is anything of worth, usefulness, or importance to you.

For Discussion

Many successful people and companies have found that prioritizing their schedules and their goals made the difference between success and failure. Prioritizing forced them to focus on first things first. Prioritizing is powerful.

If you are not putting first things first in your life and on the job, you are probably setting yourself up for failure. Your personal priorities can help guide your life. If you did not consider your priorities before going to work, it is time to consider them now.

Your top priorities usually revolve around your personal values and principles. If you took a job without knowing what is important to you, you probably will not like your job or be able to do 100 percent on the job. You risk failure on the job.

Remember: If you want to do a job and keep a job, put first things first. List your top priorities in the order of their importance, and make sure your job meets these priorities.

Presentation Suggestions

Use with Pages 20–23

Present the vocabulary aloud to the class. Display it in the room with the vocabulary words from Chapter 1. Explain that some of the words are identified later in the text of the chapter.

Print the word "PRIORITY" in the middle of the board or overhead. Move around the room and invite students to say anything they feel or think of when they hear this word. Write these in bubbles around "PRIORITY." Here is a suggested display:

Discuss as a whole group what the students' main feelings are toward priorities in their lives. Are their priorities difficult, easy, few, many, and so on? This exercise should assist you in determining the current class climate. Ask students to do the Stop and Think exercises on pages 20–22.

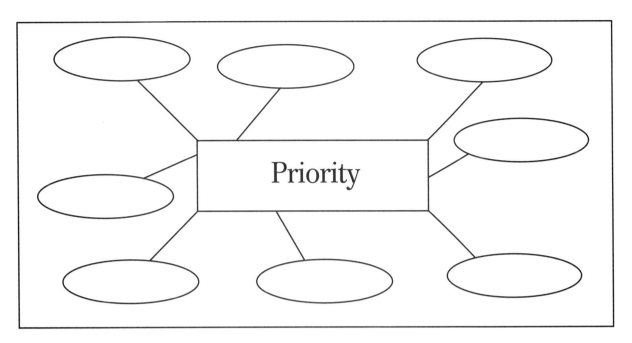

Use with Pages 23–27

Review the difference between a value and a principle. Ask a student to read paragraphs one and two of the Example on page 23. Discuss as a whole group. Ask another student to read paragraphs three and four aloud. Discuss as a whole group. Have students complete the Stop and Think exercise on page 24.

Write the following on chart paper: "Values are the main reason people work!" Post the paper in a prominent place in the classroom. Allow time for students to complete the Stop and Think on pages 25–27 individually. When this has been completed, have the class break into small groups. Have each group respond to the question, "Were you surprised by the top value on your list? Explain why or why not." Then ask one member from each group to share the group's discussion with the entire class.

Use with Pages 28–31

Invite a student to read the Examples on the bottom of page 28 aloud. Then have students quickly complete the Stop and Think on pages 29–30. Discuss the most common items chosen by the class. Ask the students for explanations and alternatives to their choices. Ask, "What would you be willing to do to overcome these obstacles?"

Discuss personal time. Ask the class to come up with its own definition of personal time. Suggest that students look ahead to pages 30–31 to create an appropriate definition. When this has been completed, write the class definition on the board or overhead and allow time for students to complete pages 30–31 individually. Ask students to return to small groups and discuss responses for approximately three minutes. Then return to the whole group and create a list of four points for each category following the format shown below. This may be done on the board, overhead, or chart paper. Then, have students copy the lists and place them in their yellow folders.

PERSONAL TIME USES

HEALTH

1. _____

2. _____

3. _____

4. _____

RELAXATION

1. _____

2. _____

3. _____

4. _____

EDUCATION

1. _____

2. _____

3. _____

4. _____

SPIRITUAL

1. _____

2. _____

3. _____

4. _____

Use with Pages 32–36

Ask how many students feel that they shoulder all the responsibilities of running the home as well as holding a job. Explain that they will now examine the idea of shared responsibilities. Encourage students to keep an open mind and a willingness to be flexible. Ask them to read and complete the Stop and Think on page 32.

Read aloud the Examples on page 33 and ask students to think back on their lives and about the good and bad changes that have occurred. Then, allow them two minutes to complete the Stop and Think on pages 33–34. Break the students into small groups and direct them to discuss their timelines with one another. If a student feels uncomfortable discussing changes in his or her life, the student can speak about someone else or listen. These discussions promote a degree of camaraderie (we're all in the same boat!) via similar experiences. Ask students to complete the Stop and Think on pages 34–35.

Ask a student to read the paragraphs under "Is Keeping Your Job a Priority?" on page 35. Emphasize the importance of maintaining a job for consecutive years. Ask, "What does holding a job for consecutive years say about you?" Accept any appropriate responses and write them on the board or overhead. Ask students for a consensus vote on the top three. Then write the top three responses on the board or overhead in the following way:

Traits of Job Keepers

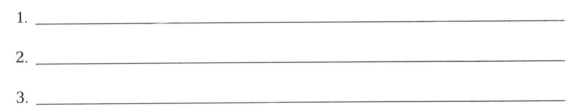

1. _____

2. _____

3. _____

Ask students to copy the above list on a sheet of paper and put the sheet into their yellow folders.

Ask students to complete the Stop and Think on pages 35–36 individually.

Until Next Time

Have you ever been told that you had a bad attitude? Do you remember an experience that triggered your attitude? Before the next class, think about how many times you may have heard words similar to those and if you ever wished you could take back something you said or did in the workplace.

Activities

Mr. Tallyman

Use: With pages 20–21

Format: Small group to whole group

Time: 15–20 minutes

Materials: Chalkboard, overhead, or chart paper; chalk or markers

1. Break the class into small groups.

2. Instruct the groups to share their reasoning behind the listing of items 1 through 10 on pages 20–21.

3. Ask the small groups to return to whole group.

4. Write the tasks in random order on the board or overhead.

5. Ask each student to read his or her list of tasks from first to last. As individuals respond, write a number on the board next to each task.

6. Next, rewrite the list to reflect the answers to step 5 above.

7. Create a permanent display entitled "PRIORITY BOARD" in the room.

8. Have students copy the list to keep in their yellow folders.

Situation Normal

Use: At the end of the chapter

Format: Small group to whole group

Time: 30–40 minutes

Materials: Copies of situation cards (text follows on next two pages), timer, pen, paper

1. Break the class into small groups.

2. Provide each group with a few instructions:

   - The activity will be improvisational role-play (make it up as you go along).

   - There are no wrong answers.

   - Be honest, not angry.

   - Some of the situations will be difficult to deal with, but so is day-to-day life.

3. Give each group a number, 1 through 5.

4. Call each group individually and read a situation card aloud to the group. Give each group a copy of their situation card.

5. Set the timer for one minute and allow the group to discuss how to role-play the situation.

6. After the minute, set the timer for three minutes and have the group role-play its reaction to the situation for the class.

7. Call "over" or "end" when three minutes are complete. The scene ends at that point.

8. After all groups are done, allow for class discussion on the use of labels in the workplace.

9. Ask, "Is your first reaction to a workplace situation always the best? What can you do to help yourself?"

Situation Cards

Situation 1

It is Tuesday afternoon in the office. You have been working hard all day. The morning had been hectic as you got your kids off to school with lunches and homework. The workday is speeding by. You have managed to catch up on the day's projects and grab a quick cup of coffee with a co-worker down the hall. As you return to your area, your boss hands you a phone message and a new project. The message is from your children's school: Your youngest daughter is sick, and the nurse wants you to pick her up. Your boss has been pleased with your work so far, but you haven't had the job for long. It is already 2 p.m., and you work until 4 p.m. School is out at 2:55 p.m., and your kids normally stay in an after-school daycare program until you pick them up at 4:20 p.m. Can your little one hold out until then? Would your boss be angry if you left? What if your boss tells you no? What are your options? What is your priority?

Situation 2

It is Thursday at 3:30 p.m. You've looked at the clock and counted the hours left in the workday. Only one-and-a-half hours to go! You are really looking forward to the date you will have in the evening. It has been a busy day with lots of customers to wait on. You are pretty sure your supervisor is pleased with your customer service. At 4:15 p.m., your supervisor swoops by and asks if you would be willing to stay until 8:00 or 9:00 p.m. to help with inventory. If you stay, you will make some extra money and a good impression. But you were really looking forward to your date. Do you stay or do you go?

Situation 3

You are expected at a job site at 8:00 a.m. When you were hired, you told the foreman your car was reliable. It was—until today. You have driven out to this distant work site every day for about a week. It is cold, damp, and windy this morning, and when you got in your car, it wouldn't start. Even though you are tired and it would be out of your way, you could take the bus to the warehouse and try to get a ride with a co-worker. That might mean you would have to return the favor someday. You could call a friend or family member, but that too might mean you would have to return a favor. Or, a day off would be nice. So what if you promised to be there every day until the job was finished? What is your priority?

Situation 4

You are so excited about your first day at your new job. It seems to be a busy, exciting work environment. You have met several co-workers and like them. As you drive to work listening to the radio and feeling successful for the first time in a long time, you pass a popular coffeehouse. The place is crowded with people. You decide that a celebration cup of coffee with other working folk sounds great! It might make you 5 or 10 minutes late, but that's not much and everyone else seems to be there. What is your priority?

Situation 5

The job has been terrific for you and for everyone associated with you. Your co-workers are good people for the most part. Your boss can be a little on the nosy side, but not aggressively so. The workers enjoy sharing conversation at lunchtime. Who doesn't? Sometimes these topics are personal; sometimes they are not. It is a relaxing part of the day. These people are almost like your friends. One afternoon a discussion leads to some personal information about a particular co-worker. You know that your supervisor would find this information very interesting. You know that this gossip will get your co-worker in trouble and maybe fired, which could get you a prime place in the office. What is your priority?

Chapter 3

Objectives

- Recognizing your attitude in the workplace.

- Noticing the effects of your attitude.

- Fixing your attitude.

Attitude

Rationale for This Topic

This is your SURVIVAL TOOL.

Your attitude can determine what you achieve in the workplace.

Good or bad, if you keep doing what you are doing, you will keep getting what you are getting.

A good attitude will help you in the workplace. A bad attitude will hurt you.

This is TRUE STUFF YOU NEED TO KNOW.

Working Vocabulary

- **Attitude.** An attitude is an automatic feeling toward something. It can also be your manner or state of mind.

- **Trait.** A trait is a personal characteristic.

For Discussion

Your attitude affects your feelings, which affect your productivity, which affects company profits. Many employers say that attitude is more important to them than work skills. Do you know why? A good employer with a good training program can usually improve your skills, but employers have little control over your attitude. Only you can control your attitude.

Now you might be saying, "My attitude is my business, and as long as I do my job, it is nobody's business but mine. Right?" Wrong! Your attitude affects your job and the people around you. Performing your job duties is only one part of being a good employee. Another important part is being an asset to your workplace. A poor attitude is not an asset. Your employer cannot afford your bad attitude. It is a risk, and others can catch it or will not want to be around you. Teamwork and customer service are important on the work site. A bad attitude hurts both, and it hurts you.

When a bad attitude works against you, you may justify it and say you are misunderstood. But this is the work site, and you must change a bad attitude to survive.

No one can have a good attitude all the time. But you can take steps to fix your attitude when needed.

Remember: Your attitude always shows. Be honest about your attitude. It is your survival tool.

Presentation Suggestions

Use with Pages 38–39

Focus attention on the definition of attitude. Allow some quiet time (5–10 minutes) for students to reflect in their own way on their attitude. This reflection may include sketching, writing, meditating, and so on. Be prepared to provide any materials necessary for the reflection choices that best fit the group. Then, have students complete the Stop and Think on pages 38–39 individually.

Use with Pages 39–45

Re-create the graphic below on the board or overhead:

KEYWORD: PRODUCTIVITY

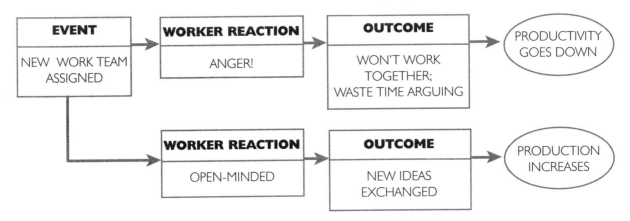

KEYWORD: PROFITS

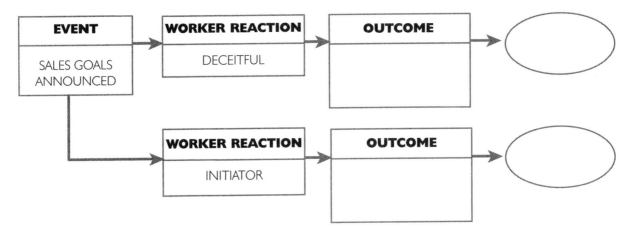

KEYWORD: COWORKERS

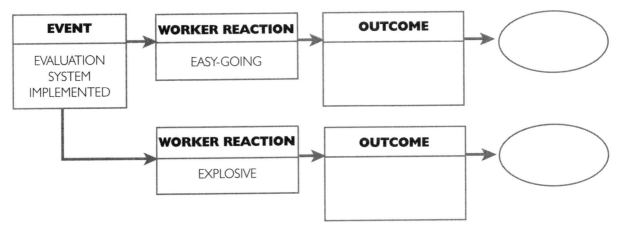

Then write the following on the board or overhead:

Attitude affects productivity, profits, and co-workers.

Ask students to give a positive outcome and a negative outcome to the worker reaction for each area mentioned. After the graphic presentation, allow time for students to break into small groups and complete the Stop and Think exercises on pages 40–41 and 42–43.

Ask the students to list ways they can tell that someone they work with has a bad attitude. These are also signs of your character and job ethics. List these on the board or overhead. Compare with the list on page 44. Then ask students to complete the Stop and Think on page 44–45 individually.

Use with Pages 45–53

Instruct students to look back at the graphic called "Which Path Is Yours?" Ask them to think about which paths they feel they take most often. Have them use these responses to help complete pages 45–48. There is little to discuss in these pages because much of the context is self-discovery. Allow as much as 25–35 minutes to complete.

Write the words "POSITIVE" and "NEGATIVE" on the board or overhead. Explain that an automatic response to something is a feeling—in other words—attitude! It is possible to concentrate on good feelings and get rid of the bad. Complete the Stop and Think on page 49 together as a whole class.

Invite a student to read aloud the bottom of page 49 about optimists and pessimists. Have the students individually complete the Stop and Think on page 50. Can being an optimist make you a happier person?

Guide the class to the "Fix Your Attitude" section. Remind students that it is possible to change a bad attitude both quickly at work and more in-depth at home. Ask a student to read the Example on page 51. Then add to the board or overhead any other appropriate suggestions the class may provide. Ask students to complete the Stop and Think exercises on pages 51–52 individually.

Have students read pages 52–53 silently and complete the Stop and Think on page 53. Give each student an index card on which to write his or her three attitude fixers. Instruct students to place the card in their yellow folders.

Until Next Time

Now that you have your attitude under control, we can move on. Have you ever felt that there was something you could do better than most people? Something you enjoy?

Something you enjoy enough to make a career out of it? Something that isn't pro basketball, pro football, actor, or recording artist? Before the next class, consider all the things you do well. Begin a mental list of these skills that you could bring with you to a job.

Activities

Situation Switch

Use: After page 48

Format: Small group to whole group

Time: 30–45 minutes

Materials: Copies of role-play cards (text given on next page)

1. Ask the class to break into small groups.

2. Pass out a role-play card to each group.

3. Allow time for each group to discuss the scene it has been given and discuss ideas on how to role-play it.

4. Have the groups turn the cards over and listen to a few directions.

5. Explain that this scene will have to be played out in two different ways—one showing a poor attitude and one portraying a good attitude.

6. Tell students that when they are not performing, they will have to pay close attention to the scene in progress.

7. When they (the audience) observe the players portraying a bad attitude, the audience will call out "switch!"

8. When "switch!" is called, the players will immediately stop.

9. The audience will then be allowed to give three positive suggestions to the players that the players must use in the rest of the scene.

10. The instructor will then say "go!" and the scene will resume using the audience's suggestions.

Role-Play Cards

Card 1

A worker is new on the job, and a co-worker is asked by the supervisor to help the new person learn the ropes.

Card 2

A supervisor tells his worker that she has to sign up for a computer class to maintain her position or to move up in the company.

Card 3

A worker had arrived late due to a child-care difficulty. The boss has met the worker on arrival to ask for an explanation.

Card 4

A supervisor has begun to ask one worker for personal information concerning another worker.

Card 5

A worker has been assigned to a committee-type team. Not all the team members know each other. Several appear to be extremely unsure of the group.

Paired Insights

Use: At the end of the chapter

Format: Pair

Time: 20 minutes

Materials: Paper and pen for notes if desired

1. Assign the students a partner (partner A and partner B).

2. Explain that each student can take notes, if desired, as the partner talks.

3. Students will discuss a time when their attitude hurt them in the workplace. Each person will have an opportunity to relate this experience to a partner.

4. Partner A will take the "helper" role first. The helper's job is to provide a sounding board and give suggestions on how to avoid or fix the attitude so that it will not become a problem in the future.

5. Partner B will talk first as partner A listens. Then the roles will change, and partner A will talk as partner B listens. (Allow approximately six minutes per person.)

6. When time is called, ask each pair to share any particularly good suggestions that came out of the exchange that could help others in the class.

Chapter 4

Objectives

- Understanding three kinds of skills.

- Seeing the importance of skills at work.

- Discovering and using your best skills.

- Improving your skills.

Skills

Rationale for This Topic

This is your SURVIVAL FOUNDATION.

You have more skills than you think you have.

You can do more than you think you can.

You are better than you think you are.

You just have to identify your skills.

This is REAL STUFF YOU NEED TO DISCOVER.

Working Vocabulary

- **Skill.** A skill is something you do well.

- **Communication.** Communication occurs when ideas are shared and understood.

- **Foundation.** The foundation is the base on which to build.

- **Opportunity.** An opportunity is a situation that can assist you in advancement.

- **Associate.** To associate is to make a meaningful, mental connection.

For Discussion

If you have never worked for a business or if it has been a long time since you worked, you may not recognize your skills. What is a skill? A **skill** is something you have the ability to do and tasks or jobs that you can do well or better than the average person.

It is important that you take this opportunity to really look at your skills. Staying on a job is much easier if you do what comes more easily and naturally to you. It is fine to try jobs that require you to learn new skills or improve weak skills. But as you start out, using skills you already have will give you a good base and allow you time to adjust to the working environment.

Presentation Suggestions

Use with Pages 55–61

Ask students to turn to pages 56–57. Allow them three to five minutes to read the list of skills and check any skills that apply. It may be necessary to explain several categories, depending on the reading levels of the students.

Examples:

- **Bookkeeping.** Keeping track of money.

- **Clerical.** Filing records, answering phones, taking messages.

- **Conflict resolution.** Solving people's problems.

- **Delegating.** Assigning duties.

- **Facilitating.** Helping with meetings and conventions.

- **Nurturing.** Being caring, nourishing, and loving.

Ask the students, "When you stopped to think about your skills, did you come up with more than you thought you had?" Discuss responses as a whole group.

Write the three types of skills on the board or overhead:

- **Performance skills** are "I can" skills—things you can do.

- **Interpersonal skills** are skills you have working with people.

- **Transferable skills** are skills that can be transferred easily to various kinds of jobs.

Ask the students to reread the definition of each type of skill as stated on page 58. Ask them to complete the Stop and Think exercises on pages 58–59.

Use with Pages 61–68

Write the words "NATURAL" and "LEARNED" on the board or overhead. Explain that a natural skill is a skill you were born with and a learned skill is, well, taught! Direct students to complete the Stop and Think on pages 61–62. Ask "Why would you want to spend time trying jobs that would require skills that are difficult for you?"

Invite a student to read the bottom of page 62 and the top half of page 63 aloud. Focus attention on the Example. Ask the students to think of people in their own lives who turned a natural ability into job success. It is a good idea to have a few stories of your own on hand in case the students are reluctant to share stories or do not know of anyone. Ask students to complete the Stop and Think on pages 63–65 individually.

Have a student read the Example on page 66 aloud. Then, solicit more examples from the students. Have students complete the Stop and Think on pages 66–68.

Use with Pages 68–76

Have students complete the Stop and Think on pages 68–69. Go on and assign the Stop and Think on page 70.

Have the students remain on page 70.

Draw a chart with these headings on the board or overhead:

Word Associated with Your Natural Skill   **Field of Work**
Specific Job

Invite a student to read the instructions at the top of page 70 aloud but do *not* have students fill in the page on their own.

Using the charts on the board, ask the students to follow the example and fill in the chart. Call on students individually to come to the board or overhead and write responses or have them respond orally as you fill in the charts.

When the students have completed both charts, allow a few minutes for them to copy their favorite responses onto page 70.

Hint: Don't prenumber the chart spaces on the board or overhead! Number as you go. This way the students will more likely give you more than six responses. They won't feel confined by a preset number of responses and will answer more freely. This will in turn provide more choices for students to use when they fill in page 70.

Have students complete pages 73–74 either individually or in groups.

Review natural and learned skill types and their definitions. Call on random students. Have the class complete the Stop and Think on pages 75–76.

Invite a student to read the bottom of page 76 aloud. Ask students to write on the backs of their yellow folders the three improvements they feel they are able to make.

Until Next Time

What jobs are you interested in that will make use of your number 1 learned skill? Check the classified advertisements or a job search Web site to get some ideas about what is available.

Activities

Three-Part Harmony (three-part activity)

Use: See below

Format: Individual

Time: Three 10-minute segments

Materials: 4-by-8 index cards (3 per student), 3-by-5 cards (18 per student), pens, board or overhead, large rubber bands, books that list many job titles and brief job descriptions. Such books include the *Occupational Outlook Handbook, The O*NET Dictionary of Occupational Titles,* and *Best Jobs for the 21st Century.*

Part I (Use after page 57)

1. Give each student three of the 4-by-8 cards.

2. Instruct the students to write the three types of skills and their definitions—one per card.

3. Explain that they will be building a card file throughout the chapter.

4. When all students have completed their cards, give each student a rubber band. Have the students place their rubber-banded cards in their yellow folders. These are their title cards.

Part II (Use after page 58)

1. Ask students to take out their 4-by-8 title cards.

2. Give each student twelve 3-by-5 index cards.

3. Have students copy their top six performance and interpersonal skills, one per card, and place them behind the title cards.

4. Instruct students to replace the rubber bands and put the cards back in their folders.

Part III (Use after page 61)

1. Ask students to take out their card file.

2. Focus attention on the transferable skill card. Invite a student to reread the definition of transferable skill aloud to the class.

3. Ask students to look at their six previously written skill cards and briefly write a description of a job that would use most of these skills.

4. Have the students mark a star at the top of the four most appealing skill cards.

5. Tell the students to move or "transfer" those starred cards behind the transferable skill title card.

6. Give the students six more 3-by-5 cards.

7. On these cards, guide students to write as many job titles as they can think of that go with each transferred skill. Direct their attention to the reference books for help.

8. The students will then be able to use this to help in future job searching.

9. Have students replace the rubber band around the card file and put it away in their yellow folders.

Job Frame-Up

Use: After page 72

Format: Individual/small group to whole group

Time: 20–25 minutes

Materials: Sunday newspaper classified ads, pens, paper, chart paper, and copy of frame diagram on the next page (one copy per student)

1. Bring in a Sunday newspaper classified ad section. Give each student a page or two of the ad section.

2. Ask students to break into small groups.

3. Ask each group to look through the ad sections to find a job description that is of interest to each individual group member. Each member chooses one job that interests him or her.

4. Each group member should write the job title on the sheet of chart paper and leave room between the job titles for more writing later.

5. Next, each group member should read aloud his or her ad. As each student reads aloud, another member should write the specific skills asked for in the ad underneath the corresponding title on the chart paper.

6. Post the finished charts in the room and discuss as a whole group.

7. Pass out a copy of the frame diagram on the next page to each student.

8. Review the directions on the diagram with the class.

9. Allow time for students to complete the diagram and ask a few to share theirs orally.

10. Have students place the finished diagrams in their yellow folders.

Frame Diagram

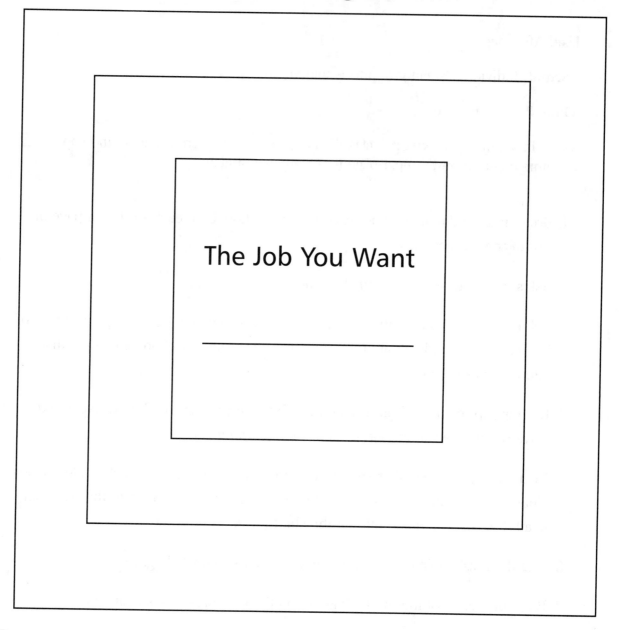

The Job You Want

_____

1. Write in the center box a job that you would like to have. Be realistic.

2. In the inner frame, write anything you are willing and able to do to reach the center.

3. In the outer frame, write what things you will do when you reach the center.

Chapter 5

Objectives

● Planning short-term goals.

● Planning long-term goals.

● Motivating yourself to reach your goals.

Goals

Rationale for This Topic

This is your SURVIVAL MAP.

Goals are important to keep you focused.

Goals point you in the direction that you want to be moving.

Want to achieve something in the next week, month, or year?
Set a goal to get you there.

It is said, "A goal is a dream with a deadline."

This is STUFF YOU NEED TO TAKE TIME TO DO.

Working Vocabulary

- **Goal.** A goal is something you are willing to work for and attain.

- **Visualize.** To visualize, you must see things in your mind like a dream.

- **Motivation.** Motivation is what makes you want to do something.

- **Accomplishment.** An accomplishment is the result of hard work. Be proud of accomplishments!

For Discussion

Goals are part of everyone's daily living. Simple goals like doing laundry on Monday or organizing your work area on Thursday are part of a weekly plan. When people accomplish things large and small, they feel better.

When you set a target and reach it, you appreciate what you've achieved much more than if someone had given you an airline ticket directly to your final destination.

A long-term career goal is important so you have a vision that will help you survive. People who have not been in the organized workforce for long are overwhelmed when asked to set goals for their future. Most are completely lost because they don't know what they want to do or can do in the working world. So a plan of action where you take one step at a time is necessary.

You need to plan short-term goals that will allow you to experience success at each step you complete. The steps are important to your long-term goal. Too many things can interfere, change, or prolong your long-term goal. It is easy to get discouraged if you do not see any possible ways for success. Everyone needs small successes. It is important that you believe your goals are good for you. Your goals should keep you in the workplace. Keeping your goals in your vision will help your job survival.

Presentation Suggestions

Use with Pages 77–80

Begin the class by reviewing the frame diagrams the students completed during the final Chapter 4 session. Use this to introduce the vocabulary. Go over the vocabulary. Then, using the completed frame diagram, ask, "On your diagram, which part is the goal? Which part shows things that motivate you? Which part shows any accomplishment? Does this help you to visualize?" Ask each question separately and accept all reasonable responses.

Show the students a United States map and ask them to think about a destination (goal) they would like to visit. Instruct them to use this goal to complete the Stop and Think exercises on pages 78–81 individually. When the students have completed the exercises, have them break into pairs or small groups to share their "trips" and outcomes, as they were able to visualize them. Call on one person per group or pair to share his or her "trip" with the entire class.

Use with Pages 81–84

Invite a student to read the Example on page 81 aloud to the class. Have students complete the Stop and Think on page 82. Discuss briefly.

Read the following to the class: William has always enjoyed drawing. He used to draw a cartoon strip for his high school newspaper. He thinks that maybe he could use his natural skill in a career. What advice would you give him about his career?

Ask for responses from the class and write these on the board. Emphasize that it may be helpful for students to consider their own goals and how they would like someone to respond.

Have students complete the Stop and Think exercises on pages 83–84. Then ask for four pairs of students to quickly role-play their advice for the entire class. One student will be the career advisor, and the other will be the person seeking advice.

Use with Pages 85–88

Explain that the students will be working with the idea of career goals, accomplishments, and motivation. Discuss the fact that career goals can be planned in the same detailed way the trip was planned.

Allow time to discuss the Stop and Think exercises on pages 85–86. Answer any questions the students may have about the completion. Provide ample time for students to thoughtfully complete the exercises.

Hint: Be certain to point out the words "ideal career" on page 85. It does not say "dream career." Steer the class away from superstar careers such as pro sports, recording artists, and so on because these are rarely attainable goals.

You will need a basketball and basket of some type for this next demonstration.

Direct attention to the bottom of page 86. Invite a student to read the text aloud for the class.

Using the basketball and basket, tell the class that your goal is to make a free-throw shot. Attempt to shoot the ball and *miss!* You have now failed at your stated goal. Ask the students for suggestions to help improve your chances of reaching your goal. Follow the suggestions until the goal is reached. Then, ask the students to turn to page 87. Discuss briefly how this page is related to the basketball demonstration. Provide the students with time to complete page 80 based on their career goals. Invite volunteers to share their goals as time allows.

Turning things around, focus attention on a successful experience from the past. Ask students to complete the Stop and Think on pages 88–89 individually.

Use with Pages 82–83

Request a student volunteer to read the Example on pages 89–90. Discuss the story. This will be familiar to some students. Ask if they can think of any other "carrots." Have them complete the Stop and Think on page 90.

Copy the carrot pattern and give one to each student. Ask the students to complete the Stop and Think on page 91. Then, pass out a carrot page to each student. Have the students rewrite the 10 things they wrote on page 91 on the carrot. Have them place the carrot in their yellow folders.

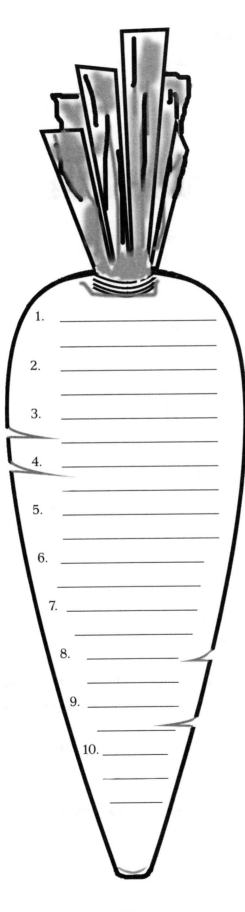

1. _____

   _____

2. _____

   _____

3. _____

   _____

4. _____

   _____

5. _____

   _____

6. _____

   _____

7. _____

   _____

8. _____

   _____

9. _____

   _____

10. _____

   _____

Until Next Time

Think about the way you react when things don't go your way. Do you run away, become aggressive, or get lazy? Have you ever tried to pass a difficulty off on someone else? Come to the next class with this in mind. You may write your response if you choose to do so.

Activities

Shape Up Your Goals

Use: After page 82

Format: Individual to small group

Time: 20–25 minutes

Materials: Large tag board cutouts of a square, rectangle, circle, triangle, and diamond; pens, blank drawing paper, tape

1. Write the word "GOAL" on the board or overhead.

2. Place the cutouts one by one on the board and hand out the blank paper.

3. Explain to students that each shape represents a goal and a way to achieve the goal.

4. Ask students to draw the shape they feel most closely represents their goal and method of achievement.

5. Then, underneath the shape, have students write a brief paragraph explaining why they chose the shape and what it represents to them.

6. When students have finished, ask them to break into small groups and allow only a few minutes to share.

7. Call on one volunteer from each group to share his or her exercise with the entire class.

8. Have the students place these sheets in their yellow folders.

Greatest Accomplishments

Use: With pages 88–89

Format: Pair

Time: 20–25 minutes

Materials: Index cards, pens, timer

1. Assign partners for the activity.

2. Explain that each student should individually think of his or her greatest accomplishment and write it on one side of the card. (Allow 2–3 minutes.)

3. Next, tell the pairs to decide which one of them is partner A and which one is partner B. Have partner B raise his or her hand.

4. Say, "Partner B will now tell partner A everything about his or her greatest accomplishment." Allow 3 minutes. When the time is over, partners switch places. Partner A tells partner B about his or her greatest accomplishment. Allow 3 minutes.

5. Now, have the partners trade cards so that A has B's card and B has A's card. Allow 6 minutes for the students to write everything they remember about their partner's greatest accomplishment. Remind them to use as many skill words as they can to describe the accomplishment.

6. Explain that students will now have the ability to see one of their accomplishments through objective eyes, such as those of an employer.

Chapter 6

Objectives

- Solving problems through time management.

- Solving problems through possibility thinking.

- Nipping small problems before they grow.

- Making backup plans.

- Finding people to discuss problems with.

Problem Solving

Rationale for This Topic

This is your SURVIVAL CHALLENGE.

Employers say problem solving seems hard for those who have not worked much or for those who are re-entering the workplace.

You face both work and personal problems. Sometimes these problems overlap or affect each other.

If you can solve your problems, you help your job survival.

This is STUFF YOU HAVE TO SOLVE.

Working Vocabulary

- **Manage.** Managing something means having control.

- **Conflict.** A conflict is a disagreement with a person or a schedule.

- **Anticipate.** If you anticipate, you look ahead.

For Discussion

Employers say problem solving seems difficult for people who have not worked or who are re-entering the work world. Many work issues that arise are simply personal problems you have not worked out.

For example, suppose your car won't start, your baby-sitter is sick, or your driver's license has expired. What do you do? A job requires a commitment of 35 to 40 hours per week, 50 weeks a year. You cannot just stay home or leave work when you want to. You must have a way to deal with expected and unexpected problems so that they do not affect your job survival.

Every person has problems both big and small. Most problems will pass in time, although they seem endless when we're going through them. Remembering that you are either part of the problem or part of the solution is helpful. Problem solving is part of everyday life. Some people have a difficult time being part of the solution. They prefer being part of the problem (doing nothing).

Presentation Suggestions

Use with Pages 94–98

Begin by introducing the vocabulary words. These are each repeated frequently throughout the chapter. Then, review the objectives. Ask the class to draw conclusions about how the words relate to the objectives.

Using the definition of manage, discuss the idea of time management. What does it mean to the students? Have them read the top of page 94 and complete the Stop and Think on pages 94–95 individually.

Ask the students, "Have you ever felt that you would be fine if there were just a few more hours in the day?" and "Have you asked yourself why you never get everything finished but others seem to manage?" Explain that the first step is to decide the best way to spend the time you have. Conduct a whole group discussion about uses of time. Draw the following diagram on the board or overhead and ask students to fill in the boxes.

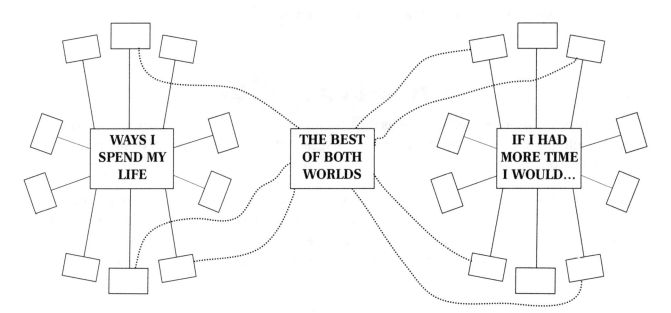

Draw connection lines between "Ways I spend my time" and "If I had more time I would..." Ask students to complete the Stop and Think exercises on pages 96–97.

Invite a student to read aloud the Example at the bottom of page 98. Review the diagram on the board or overhead and the Stop and Think on page 96 in the workbook.

Use with Pages 98–100

Have students complete the Stop and Think on pages 98–99 individually.

Direct student attention to "Method 2: Use Possibility Thinking" on page 100. Have someone read the Example on page 100. Ask the class if anyone thought about the "Until Next Time" from Chapter 5. Reread the "Until Next Time" to refresh their memories, then discuss as a whole group.

Use with Pages 101–107

Ask the students to name ways their home life affects their work. List these examples on the board or overhead. Then, ask a student to read the bottom of page 101 aloud. Next, go through the list on the board or overhead and decide whether each is a prioritizing problem, time management problem, or a communication problem. (Use abbreviations P, TM, and C.)

Ask the class to read the Example silently on page 102 and complete the Stop and Think on page 102 individually. Call on students randomly to listen to responses.

Move on to "Method 3: Solve Small Problems Before They Grow" on page 103. Have a student read the top of page 103.

Write "SOLVING PROBLEMS" at the top of the board or overhead. Then list the three methods as follows:

Method 1: Time Management

Method 2: Possibility Thinking

Method 3: Solve Small Problems

As you write them, review the theory behind each method.

Ask the class for examples from real life of how small problems grow into large ones. Allow time for discussion. Be sure to ask students if these are home or work problems. Encourage students to use these examples to begin the Stop and Think on pages 103–104.

Now, ask for a student to describe Method 1 and give an example of how it works. Continue in the same way with Methods 2 and 3. Introduce the section "Method 4: Make a Backup Plan." Ask a student for his or her definition of a backup plan. Write it on the board or overhead. Complete the Stop and Think on page 105 together as a class. Discuss.

The section on "Method 5: Talk About Your Problems" is more personal for the students. Explain that it is always a good idea to have someone to talk to and to vent their problems with. Frustrations will not bottle up and explode.

Be, however, sure to emphasize that work is work and home is home. So everyone should have someone to talk about home problems with and someone else to talk about work problems with.

Provide each student with an index card on which to write the following:

REMEMBER

INSIDE PROBLEMS—KEPT INSIDE!

OUTSIDE PROBLEMS—KEPT OUTSIDE!

Have students complete the Stop and Think exercises on pages 106–107 individually.

Until Next Time

Has anyone ever told you about a habit you had? What was the habit? Do you currently have any habits that could be a problem in the workplace? What would you do if a co-worker had an annoying habit that constantly bothered you at work? Think about it until next time.

Activities

Time Flies

Use: After page 97

Format: Small group to whole group

Time: 15 minutes

Materials: Chart paper, markers

1. Present the idea of two types of time: free time and productive time. During free time we do what we want. During productive time we do what we must, such as work, laundry, and so on. In this activity the concentration is on productive time.

2. Break the class into small groups.

3. Give each group a sheet of chart paper and markers. Instruct the groups to write "PRODUCTIVE TIME" in the center of the paper and draw a rectangle around it.

4. The students should then write all the productive time uses they can think of in the area around the words "PRODUCTIVE TIME."

5. Next, call on a representative of each group to present the group's "PRODUCTIVE TIME" to the class.

You Can Do This!

Use: With pages 100–101

Format: Small group

Time: 15–20 minutes

Materials: Chart paper, pens, and workbook pages 100–101

1. Ask a student to read aloud the top of page 100 and the Example.

2. Write "POSSIBLE" on the board or overhead.

3. Say, "This is the word *possible*. It means that something can be done. When you use possibility thinking, you remain positive and open. Your attitude is good, and you begin to believe you can do something!"

4. Write "YOU CAN DO THIS!" on the board or overhead.

5. Divide the class into three groups.

6. Give each group chart paper and pens.

7. Assign each group one of the Stop and Think questions on pages 100–101.

8. Allow discussion time for the groups and have them write their responses to the question they were assigned on the chart paper.

9. Call on each group individually to answer the questions.

Chapter 7

Objectives

- Recognizing your good and bad habits.

- Seeing effects of habits in your work life.

- Seeing effects of habits in your personal life.

- Changing bad habits and establishing more good habits.

Habits

Rationale for This Topic

This is your SURVIVAL GUIDE.

It is hard to recognize your own habits.

Habits are so much a part of you that you do not see them as habits.

You do not see their effects on your working life. Do not underestimate the effects of good and bad habits.

Many habits are connected to character traits.

This STUFF BELONGS TO YOU.

Working Vocabulary

- **Habit.** A habit is a constant, often unconscious behavior pattern acquired by frequent repetition.

- **Excuse.** An excuse is a reason used to justify doing or not doing something.

- **Image.** An image is the way people see you.

For Discussion

Our habits are difficult to admit. It is sometimes hard to recognize your own habits because they are so much a part of you.

We all form habits. Some are good, and some are bad. How many habits do you have? These are things you do repeatedly and often without realizing it. Do they make you look good or bad? Are they healthy or unhealthy? Are they safe or unsafe? Do you do them every day? How long have you had your habits? Which habits would you like to keep and which would you like to throw away?

Bad habits can make you look bad in and out of the workplace. Bad habits are not good for you, show lack of discipline, make negative statements about you, and work against you. Good habits do just the opposite.

Old, bad habits are hard to throw away. You may not realize that they have always caused you problems and have been the basis of trouble. They are trouble and must go. How can you begin to change your bad habits? You must change them to survive on the job.

Presentation Suggestions

Use with Pages 110–113

Begin by discussing the three vocabulary words. Ask the students to provide real-life examples of each word. Discussing each word separately may do this most effectively. Then, ask a student to read aloud the Example on page 110. Allow time for students to complete the Stop and Think on pages 110–111 individually.

Briefly discuss the difference between bad habits and good habits. Ask for examples from the class. Write several on the board under the headings "GOOD HABITS" and "BAD HABITS" as shown below:

BAD HABITS	GOOD HABITS
1.	1.
2.	2.
3.	3.
4.	4.
5.	5.

Next, have students complete the Stop and Think on pages 112–113 individually. Remind students that everyone has bad habits. They should not feel embarrassed by them, especially if they are willing to change.

Use with Pages 113–110

Ask the class, "Why do people encourage good habits? Who do you know that has encouraged you to develop good habits in the past?" Briefly discuss the Stop and Think on pages 113–114. Talk about the teacher image that is used. Then break the class into small groups to complete the Stop and Think on pages 113–114. When completed (approximately 10 minutes), ask for group representatives to give examples of their group's responses.

Continue by assigning the self-test on pages 115–117. (Allow 20–25 minutes to complete.)

When students are done, return to the GOOD HABITS/BAD HABITS listing on the board. Continue to list several more bad habits. Then, for the middle section of the board or overhead, ask the students to think of ways they could change the bad habits into good habits. Your list may look something like this:

BAD HABITS	CHANGES MADE	GOOD HABITS
1. Never completes homework.	1. Brings books home.	1. Always has homework.
2. Temperamental.	2. Takes deep breaths before speaking.	2. Thinks before speaking.
3. Was a follower.	3. Volunteers for lead position.	3. Thinks for yourself.
4.	4.	4.
5.	5.	5.

Use with Pages 118–121

Ask the students for one or two examples of a time when they tried to make an excuse to cover for a bad habit. What happened to them? How did they feel about covering for the habit?

Remind the students that the way they felt means that the bad habit had an effect on their personal life. Have them complete the Stop and Think on page 118 individually.

Discuss with the class the image of bad feelings as baggage, something that weighs your spirit down. Ask, "How many have heard this comparison before? In what context?" After a discussion, ask students to complete the Stop and Think on page 119.

Ask a student to read aloud the text on page 120 under "Good Habits in Your Personal Life." Talk with the class about the fact that good habits, just like bad habits, follow from personal life to work life. Sometimes it may even be the same habit, but it causes different problems in different places. Consider a board or overhead presentation as shown below:

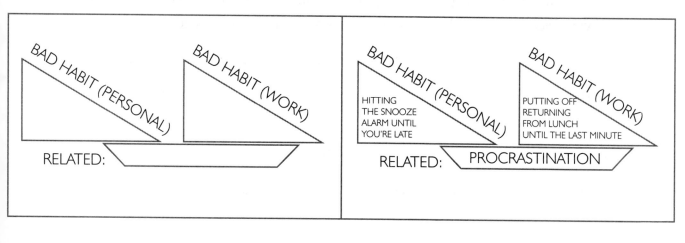

Direct the students to complete the Stop and Think exercises on pages 120–121.

Use with Pages 115–118

Talk about the meaning of achievement. Have the students identify general achievements such as graduating, buying a car, buying a house, and finding a good job. Then, discuss the idea that achievements don't always have to be big things. They could be something as simple as getting to this class every week or getting up on time every morning. Next, direct students to complete the Stop and Think on pages 122–123.

Invite a student to read the text on pages 123–125 aloud. Then complete the Stop and Think together as a whole class.

Until Next Time

Beside habits, many things make outward statements to other people. Manners are one of them. What do you consider to be good manners and what do you consider to be bad manners? Think about it until next time.

Activities

Don't Be a Bin Hog with Baggage

Use: With pages 119–120

Format: Individual to whole group

Time: 10–15 minutes

Materials: Pen/pencil, copies of template on next page

1. After the class completes the Stop and Think exercises on pages 119–120, provide each student with a copy of the template on the next page.

2. Have students write their "baggage" on the travel stickers on the front.

3. Have them write a way to leave the "baggage" behind on the items on the unpacked side.

4. Allow time for voluntary sharing as a whole class.

5. Have students place their "suitcases" in their yellow folders.

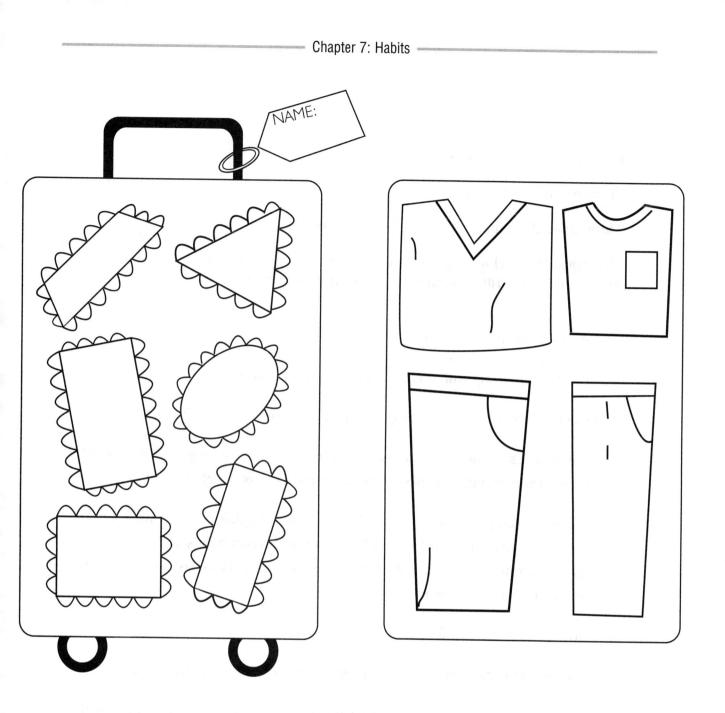

NAME:

It Seems That

Use: After pages 123–125

Format: Pair to whole group

Time: 25–30 minutes

Materials: White chart paper or poster board; pens; pencils; markers; 6 index cards with a "G" written on them and 6 with a "B" written on them.

1. Break the students into pairs.

2. Provide each group with a chart paper or poster board.

3. Direct attention back to the Stop and Think on pages 123–125.

4. Explain that students will be drawing a workspace that belongs to someone. They are to include as many details about the workspace as possible.

5. Next, give each pair of students a "G" or "B" card. Explain that "G" means that they are to illustrate a workspace of a person with good habits and "B" means that they are to illustrate a workspace that shows bad habits. Ask students not to show their cards to other pairs.

6. Allow 20–25 minutes for students to design and draw.

7. When students have finished, ask several pairs to show their drawings.

8. Ask the class to respond to each drawing by stating what they can tell about the person who works in the space.

Chapter 8

Objectives

- Understanding what manners are.

- Identifying good and bad manners.

- Noticing the effects of manners.

- Learning the magic of good manners.

Manners

Rationale for This Topic

This is your SURVIVAL ENHANCER.

Manners make a statement about you instantly.

Manners are a form of communication that we rarely think about. But everyone observes your manners.

Something happens when you practice good manners. I call it magic.

This is STUFF YOU NEED TO REALIZE.

Working Vocabulary

- **Manners.** Manners are a way of acting. Manners are a person's bearing or behavior.

- **Enhance.** Something is enhanced when it is made better.

For Discussion

Manners make a statement about you instantly. We may rarely think about our manners, but everyone we come in contact with observes them.

Bad manners may not destroy your skills, education, or qualifications for a job, but they certainly make you look bad. They certainly make a statement about you. Bad manners can disrupt a workplace, interfere in job progression, and hurt your ability to create an opportunity in the work world.

Good manners show good sense and are impressive. People like good manners. Everyone can become skilled in good manners regardless of gender, economic level, background, race, environment, or disability. Good manners are assets that work in your favor for job survival.

Something happens when you practice good manners. I call it magic.

Presentation Suggestions

Use with Pages 128–133

Ask the students to respond to "Until Next Time" from Chapter 7. It will be helpful to reread the section in case many have forgotten the theme.

Invite a student to read the Example on page 128 aloud. Discuss and then have the group complete the Stop and Think on pages 128–129. Allow time for a whole group discussion. Have students read the bottom of page 129 silently and complete the Stop and Think on page 130 individually. Discuss the contrast between what the students wrote on pages 128–129 and page 130. Ask, "If a potential employer were talking about you after an interview, how many positive things about your manners would he or she say? Is it possible to correct or relearn manners as an adult?" Discuss all appropriate responses.

Invite a student to read the Example on page 131. Ask, "How did good manners help Carmen? Give examples from the story that show proof of good manners." Next, break the class into small groups to complete the Stop and Think on page 132. When the students finish, ask for volunteers to share their group's responses.

Ask the students to read the text on the bottom of page 132 silently. Call on a student to read aloud the Example on page 133. Ask, "In what ways was Elsa rude? How did this put her job in jeopardy?" Discuss appropriate responses. As a whole group, complete the Stop and Think on pages 133 and discuss responses. You may choose to compare and contrast the exercises on pages 132 and 133 on the board or overhead as shown below:

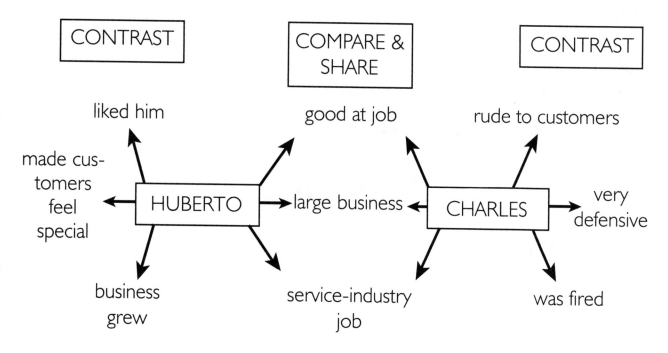

Use with Pages 134–137

Read aloud "Good Manners Versus Bad Manners" on page 134 to the class. Discuss the scenario of a first date. Perhaps invite a few first date stories from the students if time allows. Then, ask the students to find a partner (or assign partners) to complete the Stop and Think on pages 134–135. It might be fun for the students to expand this exercise by drawing an index card with either the word "GREAT" or "DISGUSTING" written on it. They could then role-play a brief first date scene using their information from pages 127–128.

Remind the students that a first date is not the only time good manners impress people. Good manners take self-awareness and work, but in the workplace they are always welcome and worthwhile. Have students complete the Stop and Think on page 136 individually. Share responses as a whole class. When the students have finished, have them go directly to the Stop and Think on page 137 and complete it individually.

Use with Pages 138–141

Request a student to read aloud the Example on page 138. Ask, "What suggestions would you give the supervisor if he asked you for help in handling the situation?" Have the students find a partner for completing the Stop and Think on pages 138–139. Discuss the students' responses.

Ask the class to read page 139 silently and complete the Stop and Think on pages 139–140. Allow time for volunteers to share their stories with the class.

Explain that the Stop and Think on pages 140–141 is a self-test. Have students complete it individually and place completed pages in their yellow folders.

Until Next Time

Think about the ways you are able to tell what your job responsibilities are. Have you ever had a job where you were hired to do one main thing but were also responsible for several other things? Be prepared to give examples in class next time.

Activities

Complimentary, My Dear

Use: After page 133

Format: Whole group

Time: 20 minutes

Materials: Students' names on slips of paper, jar, pen, paper

1. Say, "What is one thing that shows good manners and can make someone's day? What makes people work harder? What makes people feel special and important? Compliments! They are often the key to making people feel better about themselves and you."

2. Arrange the chairs in a circle.

3. Discuss the following questions and the supplemental information included after this activity.

- What is a compliment?

- What are some types of compliments? Think of something you or someone else has been complimented on and share it.

- Why do we like to receive compliments?

- Why is it good to give compliments?

- How can compliments demonstrate good manners?

- Why is it important to be a gracious receiver of compliments?

4. Have each student draw a name from the jar and write a short, complimentary note to that person.

5. Have the students try to think of a positive thing they could say to someone they haven't been getting along with.

Supplemental Information

- A **compliment** is an expression of esteem, respect, affection, or admiration (Webster's).

- **Tips on giving compliments:**

  - Be sincere.

  - Honesty is the best policy.

  - Use eye contact.

  - Personalize by giving different compliments for different people.

  - A written compliment counts double.

- **Types of compliments:**

  - Appearance

  - Personality

- Characteristics

- Values/beliefs

- Work done well

- **Tips for receiving compliments:**

  - Thank the person for the compliment.

  - Accept it graciously.

  - Smile.

  - Use eye contact.

  - Return the compliment with a compliment.

Heart of the Matter

Use: After page 137

Format: Group of two or three

Time: 25–30 minutes

Materials: Index cards, pen, paper

1. Explain that this activity is a role-play and will be done in groups of two or three, depending on the card that is drawn.

2. Have index cards laid face down on the desk or table. On the front should be written one of the following sets of information. Be sure to have these cards repeated enough so that every student is involved in a presentation.

Setting: A job interview

People: Two

Manners: Good

Setting: A job interview

People: Two

Manners: Bad

Setting: A meeting with management

People: Three

Manners: Good

Setting: A meeting with management

People: Three

Manners: Bad

---

3. Ask a student to choose a card. When the student has looked at the information, he or she may choose the group members.

4. The students should write a script that portrays the setting and manners described on the card.

5. Finally, the students should perform the skits for the entire class.

Chapter 9

Objectives

- Knowing your primary job responsibility.

- Knowing your secondary job responsibility.

- Understanding the structure of the workplace.

- Seeing where workers fit in the structure of the workplace.

- Understanding the importance of your job.

Job Responsibilities

Rationale for This Topic

This is your SURVIVAL INSURANCE.

Your primary job responsibility is what you were hired to do.

Other jobs you do on the work site are secondary.

The only person who can change this is your manager or assistant manager.

Your primary responsibility can make a difference in profits.

This is STUFF YOU MUST KNOW.

Working Vocabulary

- **Responsibility.** Taking responsibility means that you accept positive and negative aspects of a job.

- **Primary.** Anything that is primary comes first or most often.

- **Secondary.** Anything that is secondary comes after others or less often.

- **Distraction.** A distraction can draw attention away from what you are doing.

- **Focus.** When you have focus, your attention is on what you are doing.

For Discussion

Do you know your own job responsibilities? Your primary job responsibility is what you were hired to do. Any other job you perform on the work site is secondary. Only your manager or assistant manager can change this.

Do you know the job responsibilities of the people in your workplace? If you do not understand the structure of your work site, then you cannot understand what part each job function plays in the total success of the business. You cannot understand how the business makes a profit and how each job affects profit. If a business does not make a profit, there will be no job for you. Until you put the total picture together, your job is just a job and not a part of the business success. It has no importance to you.

It takes teamwork to make a business successful. People work together for a common goal. Knowing why your job is important to the team and the big picture can make you feel good about what you do.

Presentation Suggestions

Use with Pages 143–150

Discuss the vocabulary words. Be certain the students are clear on the difference between primary and secondary responsibilities.

Read the top of page 143 aloud to the class. Then ask the students to find partners and complete the Stop and Think exercises on pages 143–146.

Upon completion of the Stop and Think exercises, ask students to discuss their responses. Address any differences that occur due to personal interpretation. Remind the students that personal interpretation differences are the main reason to ask employers for clarification of primary and secondary responsibilities if necessary.

Invite a student to read aloud the Example on page 147. As the student reads, write the workplace structure on the board or overhead in a schematic manner, as shown in the following example:

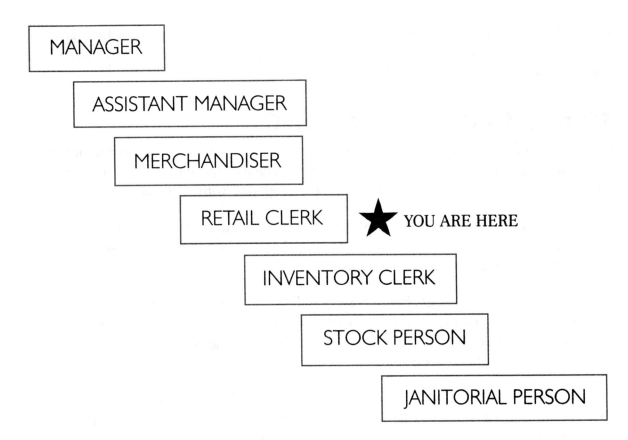

Use schematic maps to complete the Stop and Think on page 147 as a class.

Then have students complete the Stop and Think on page 148 individually. For students who are currently unemployed, assist them in deciding on a job title that interests them. Discuss these together as a whole group. You may invite student volunteers to draw their structure setups on the board or overhead before or during the discussion. Students should place a copy of their workplace structure schematic maps in their yellow folders.

Have the students complete the Stop and Think on page 149. Emphasize how it is the employee's responsibility to know their primary and secondary job duties. Ask the students if they've ever taken jobs where the duties wound up being different from what they thought they would be.

Use with Pages 148–150

Refer to the workplace structures as a student reads the bottom of page 148 and top of page 149.

Have students complete the Stop and Think on page 149. Encourage the students to share their responses orally.

Review the definition of secondary jobs. Write it on the board. Then direct the class to complete the Stop and Think on page 150 individually. Ask for volunteers to share their responses when they have finished.

Use with Pages 144–146

Emphasize to the students that teamwork is important in all workplaces. Sometimes these are formally assigned teams formed to address a specific purpose or need. Sometimes they are simply a workplace where people must cooperate with each other.

Invite a student to read the top of page 151 aloud. Ask students to complete the Stop and Think exercises on pages 151–152 individually. These two exercises are closely related. Then discuss both exercises as a whole group.

Review the definition of "goal" from Chapter 5. Read the top of page 153 to the class. Ask for students to provide examples from real life that illustrate how someone on a team—in a workplace or involved in a sport—may have distracted others on the team and prevented them reaching a goal. Share and discuss.

Have students complete the Stop and Think on page 153 individually. Provide each student with a 4-by-8 index card. On the blank side have them write "GOALS." On the lined side, have them copy their responses from page 153. Have them place the cards in their yellow folders.

Until Next Time

Before the next class, think about all the places where you must follow a specific set of rules. How do you feel about rules? Are rules the same as rights? Is there a difference between legal rights and given rights? Think about these questions until next time.

Activities

Classified Responsibilities

Use: After page 150

Format: Individual

Time: 20 minutes

Materials: Pens; paper; highlighter; ads for job openings from newspapers, the Internet, or other source

1. Explain to the class that the activity deals with identification of both primary and secondary job responsibilities.

2. Provide each student with two ads for job openings.

3. Tell the students to use their highlighters to identify the primary responsibility in the advertisement and to use their pens to circle the secondary responsibilities.

4. Next, have students write a job description for one of the advertised jobs. This job description would be one that an employer would give to a potential employee.

5. The students may read these descriptions aloud and have other students identify the primary and secondary responsibilities from their job descriptions.

   This activity may be expanded as follows:

6. Then ask the students to write a classified advertisement for a job of their choice. The ad must include one primary responsibility and three secondary responsibilities.

7. Post these ads in the classroom.

I Will Survive Crossword

Use: At end of chapter

Format: Individual

Time: 20 minutes

Materials: Pencils, copies of crossword puzzle

1. Give each student a copy of the puzzle on the facing page.

2. Make sure everyone understands the directions.

3. Collect and check the puzzles when everyone is done. The answer key follows the puzzle.

I Will Survive

Name: _____

Directions: Complete the crossword puzzle below.

Across

7. Job duty

9. Impression made

10. Make better

11. A constant behavior

12. A defensive explanation of what you did or didn't do

Down

1. To look forward to

2. A disagreement

3. First things first

4. Takes attention away from your work

5. Concentration

6. A way of acting

8. Have control

I Will Survive Answer Key

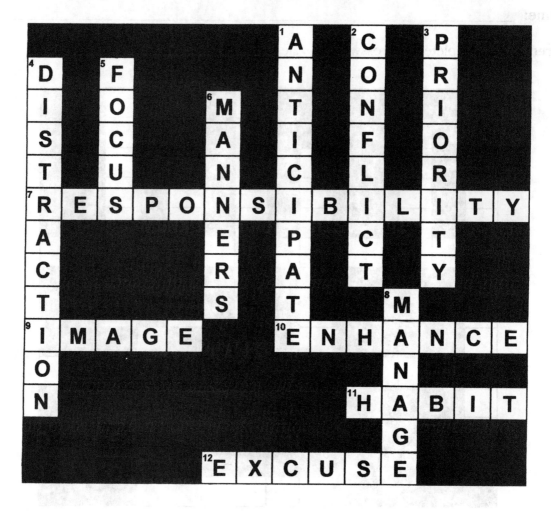

Chapter 10

Objectives

- Understanding that every workplace has rules.

- Understanding the difference between spoken and unspoken rules.

- Seeing the importance of rules in the workplace.

- Knowing the difference between legal rights and given rights.

House Rules and Rights

Rationale for This Topic

This is your SURVIVAL ADVANTAGE.

Every business has written rules and regulations.

But it is the spoken and unspoken rules that can cause you trouble.

Every employee has lawful and given rights.

Caution: Know what is a lawful right and what is a given right before you speak.

This is STUFF THAT WILL COST YOU YOUR JOB OR ADVANCEMENT.

Working Vocabulary

- **Rules.** Rules are statements of expected behavior.

- **Lawful rights.** Lawful rights or legal rights are rights you are entitled to by law.

- **Given rights.** Given rights are rights and privileges that your employer or manager grants to you.

For Discussion

Every business has rules and regulations. One example is safety rules, which are very clear and regulated by a government agency. Another example is company rules, which are written and always available for review. Company rules are also covered during new employee orientation.

It is the rules that are not written that can cause trouble for workers. These rules are sometimes spoken and sometimes unspoken, but they are still house rules. Have you heard the saying, "Rules are made to be broken"? For job survival, never stretch or break the rules, especially on the work site.

You also have rights in the workplace. Some of these rights are granted by law. Some are privileges given to you by your employer. For example, protection against discrimination is a legal right. But allowing casual dress at work is something your employer decides. Be sure you know what is a legal right and what is an employer-granted privilege before you say that your rights are being violated in the workplace. This is your survival advantage.

Presentation Suggestions

Use with Pages 155–161

Begin by asking the class to read silently the first paragraph on page 155. Then ask, "What is one of the main reasons companies have rules and regulations? When do most companies present rules to employees? Why do you think companies choose this time to make employees familiar with their rules and regulations?" Discuss the responses to these questions. Then have students complete the Stop and Think on page 155. Discuss answers as a whole group.

Ask the class to read the first paragraph on page 149 silently. Ask, "What is the difference between spoken rules and written rules, aside from the fact that one is written down?"

Have students complete the Stop and Think on pages 146–157 individually, and discuss responses as a class.

Ask a student to read aloud the paragraph under "Unspoken Rules" page 157. Next, have that student list the three types of rules. Write these on the board or overhead as shown below. Call on students to write a definition of each underneath the rule type. Then, call on other students to write examples in the correct columns. Add as many examples as will fit.

WRITTEN RULES	SPOKEN RULES	UNSPOKEN RULES
Definition:	Definition:	Definition:
Example:	Example:	Example:
Example:	Example:	Example:

Provide each student with a 4-by-8 index card. Allow time for the class to copy the information from the board or overhead on the card. Students may place these cards in their yellow folders as a quick reference.

Have students complete the Stop and Think on pages 157–158 individually. Read the "Things You Would Report" section aloud with the class. Divide the class into small groups to complete the Stop and Think on pages 158–159. When the students have completed their exercise in the groups, go around the room and make a tally of yes and no answers for each situation. Ask the groups to share portions of their discussions throughout the tallying process.

Have the students read the Example on pages 159–160 silently. Then ask these questions:

- What rule was Carla breaking?

- What type of rule was it?

- Why would an employer want to enforce a rule like this? Provide some reasons.

Invite a student to read aloud the paragraphs under the Example on page 160. Have students complete the Stop and Think exercises on pages 160–161 individually. Follow with a whole group discussion.

Use with Pages 161–165

Write the words "LAWFUL RIGHTS" and "GIVEN RIGHTS" on the board or overhead, or direct student attention back to the vocabulary. Ask a student to read the definitions and examples of each type of right provided on page 161. Have students complete the Stop and Think on page 162 individually. Discuss responses as a whole group. List as many responses on the board or overhead as possible. Be sure the students are clear about who is responsible for knowing legal rights and given rights. Complete the Stop and Think exercises on pages 163–164 together as a class. Allow plenty of time to read the situations aloud and to discuss the questions and answers. This may take some time!

Continue on after the discussion and allow the class no more than 1 minute to check off the rights on page 158. Read off each right. Ask "Is this a legal right?" Ask students to raise their hands if they agree. Ask if the same right is a given right. Ask students to raise their hands if they agree. Discuss any discrepancies.

Until Next Time

Consider the role that stress plays in your life. What are some things that stress you out? Have you ever thought about trying to turn those stressful things into the very things that motivate you? Think about it until next time.

Activities

Survival Search

Use: At end of chapter

Format: Individual

Time: 20 minutes

Materials: Pencils, copies of word-search puzzle on next page

1. Give each student a copy of the puzzle.

2. Make sure everyone understands the directions.

3. Collect and check the puzzles when everyone is done.

Job Survival

Name: _____

Directions: Find and circle the words listed below. The words are listed horizontally, vertically, and diagonally.

G	N	I	T	H	G	I	F	Z	I	Z	R	D	U	U
K	S	E	C	N	E	U	Q	E	S	N	O	C	S	L
M	M	Z	T	K	D	C	H	O	I	C	E	S	S	Q
E	O	Q	S	N	O	I	T	A	U	L	A	V	E	D
F	O	C	O	M	P	L	I	M	E	N	T	S	R	K
U	R	I	G	H	T	S	E	E	L	H	E	O	D	L
N	T	D	V	K	F	N	C	F	F	T	V	U	L	L
S	S	N	O	I	T	A	L	U	G	E	R	A	A	E
P	E	M	R	A	L	E	A	I	R	L	G	W	U	A
O	R	E	T	P	X	D	V	T	D	E	N	W	S	T
K	D	I	K	T	R	E	I	H	L	P	I	V	A	I
E	O	R	I	E	N	M	V	L	J	H	W	B	C	N
N	O	M	J	M	E	T	R	S	M	O	K	I	N	G
W	E	S	O	O	H	C	U	T	H	N	B	O	E	W
E	N	D	U	B	Q	Y	S	A	F	E	T	Y	L	R

Casualdress	Fighting	Restroom
Choices	Fired	Rights
Choose	Flextime	Safety
Compliments	Given	Smoking
Consequences	Job	Survival
Documentation	Legal	Telephone
Eating	Overtime	Unspoken
Evaluations	Regulations	Workplace

Job Survival Answer Key

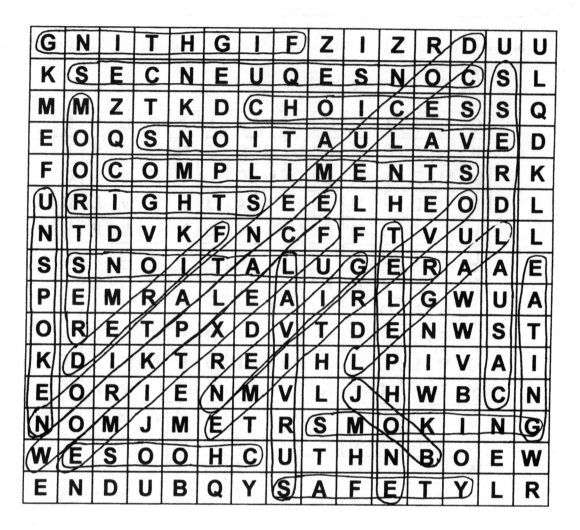

The Three Cs

Use: At end of chapter

Format: Small group

Time: 30 minutes

Materials: Chart paper, pens, pencils, and situation cards

1. Divide the class into small groups.

2. Say to the class, "We have spent a lot of time talking about legal and given rights, but also about choices and consequences. You must make decisions based on your knowledge of legal and given rights. Imagine that you go back to your car after class. When you open your door, you're shocked to see a huge rattlesnake sitting in the driver's seat. What would you do?"

3. Before students answer the question, tell them you want to hear what they would do step by step. For example, "First I would close the door, then I would…"

4. No matter how simple or complex the answer, explain to the students that they used a decision-making strategy to figure out what to do. Tell the students that most people use a strategy even if they don't realize it.

5. Teach the students a simple decision-making process by remembering the three Cs: choices, consequences, and choose.

6. Explain the following or write them on the board or overhead.

   ● Step 1: Choices. Think or make a list of all the choices available to you. Another word for choices is alternatives.

   ● Step 2: Consequences. Think of all the possible consequences, both positive and negative, for each choice. Be sure to consider the consequences for you and other people involved.

   ● Step 3: Choose. Look at all of the consequences and decide which will have the most satisfactory results for you.

7. Give each group a situation from the next page and have the group members go through the three-C process.

8. Have them write down the three Cs on the chart paper, followed by lists based on their group's situation. Finally, tell each group to reach a decision.

9. Have students share how they handled their situations.

Situation Cards

Situation 1

You have been feeling poorly all morning and think it may be slowing you down. Sometimes a clear soft drink helps to settle your stomach, but your company doesn't allow soft drinks on the work site. What do you do?

Situation 2

A co-worker who is a friend of yours routinely clocks in 10 to 15 minutes late in the morning and clocks out 10 to 15 minutes early in the evening. When asked about it by a supervisor, your friend says he takes only 30 minutes for lunch as part of flexible time. You know this is untrue. Do you report it?

Situation 3

In the summer months, your company has a casual dress policy. You really want to wear shorts but are not sure if that is acceptable. The company seems very conservative, so you think shorts are probably not acceptable. But you really want to wear shorts. What do you do?

Situation 4

You've never had access to an Internet e-mail account. The company policy is to use e-mail for business only, but you and many co-workers use it a few times a week for personal communications. Who watches anyway? What do a few notes to friends hurt? Do you continue or stop?

Situation 5

In nearly a year of work, you have received highly complimentary evaluations. Your co-workers like you, and you're very proud of your success. One afternoon you're called into your supervisor's office and told that you must pack your things—you've been fired! You are shocked! You ask for documentation and reasons. Your employer says your recent work has been unsatisfactory, and that's it! What do you do?

Chapter 11

Objectives

- Understanding stress in the workplace.

- Identifying good and bad stress.

- Changing bad stress.

- Evaluating your job stress.

- Changing overpowering stress to empowering stress.

Job Stress

Rationale for This Topic

This is your SURVIVAL SECRET.

You cannot avoid job stress in the workplace.

Good stress pumps you up, and bad stress drains you.

Bad stress can be overpowering.

If you have a job that is overpowering your life, something must change.

This is STUFF YOU CANNOT IGNORE.

Working Vocabulary

- **Stress.** Stress is a mentally or emotionally disruptive influence.

- **Overpower.** Anything that appears too large or difficult to deal with may overpower you.

- **Empower.** Anything that gives you the feeling that you are successful and in control empowers you.

For Discussion

You cannot avoid stress on the job. Good job stress pumps you up, and bad stress drains you. If the demands of a job are so strong that they overpower you, you must make changes. Either you take another job or work on changing the stress. If you want to keep your job and are working toward your long-term goals, then work on reducing your stress.

How do you lessen stress on the job? Identify what is causing you the greatest stress. Is it your boss, co-workers, personal problems, lack of skills, health, lack of time, fatigue, or something else? This is the start of your stress reduction.

Presentation Suggestions

Use with Pages 167–172

Begin by displaying and introducing the vocabulary words. Have the class read the top of page 167 silently. Next, write the points from the Example on the board or overhead. Ask the students to add to the list of job stresses. Have students complete the Stop and Think on pages 167–168 individually. Share responses as a whole class. Then read page 168 silently.

Ask the students to name ways stress can affect you. Discuss the difference between good and bad stress, as well as what makes it good or bad.

Have students complete the Stop and Think on pages 168–169. When the students have finished, invite them to share stories from their lives about when these stresses have affected them.

Review the definition of overpower. Have students complete the Stop and Think on page 170 individually and discuss it as a whole group.

Ask the students if they truly believe that bad stress can be changed to good or motivating stress. Briefly discuss. Ask students to quickly complete the Stop and Think on page 171 individually. Then ask a student to read the paragraphs underneath the Stop and Think aloud on pages 171–172.

Use with Pages 172–170

Direct students to complete the Stop and Think on page 172 individually. (For students currently unemployed, suggest they consider their most recent job or one they have interviewed for.) Have students tear out page 172 and place it in their yellow folders.

Direct the class to move immediately to the Stop and Think on pages 174–175. Have students complete it individually. Allow time to divide students into small groups to discuss their responses. Some students may be able to share personal experiences that address questions 1–4.

Ask a student to read aloud "Turn Overpowering Stress into Empowering Stress" on page 175. Have students discuss and then complete the Stop and Think on page 176. Allow time for students to share voluntarily with the whole class. Ask, "When is it important to change overpowering stress?"

Divide students into small groups to complete the Stop and Think on page 177. When the groups have finished, ask a group representative to share the group's suggestions. Write these on the board or overhead and allow time for discussion.

Activities

Difficult Situations

Use: At end of chapter

Format: Individual to whole group

Time: 20–30 minutes

Materials: Paper, pens, pencils

1. Say to the class, "Today we are going to role-play difficult situations at work and brainstorm ways of resolving problems. We have had many situations throughout this course, and you may draw on any of those experiences for this activity."

2. Ask each student to think of a difficult encounter he or she has seen or experienced at work. Students may make up a situation if they prefer.

3. Have the students write out each scenario in two or three lines without using real names. For example:

- Mary came up to my desk and asked me where her watch was. I said I didn't know. Then she accused me of stealing it.

- I'm working on a team project with two other guys, but they don't want to do any work. Since I don't want to be fired, I am doing all the work.

4. Collect the scenarios.

5. Divide the class into small groups and give a scenario to each person at random. Together, the group must come up with a way to handle each of the situations. The group can create a new scenario if it is given one that is unrealistic.

6. Have group members present their solutions to the rest of the class. Discuss the solutions. Were they appropriate? Realistic? Does everyone agree on the solution? Would you probably handle things differently if you were older or younger?

Job Stress Crossword

Use: At end of chapter

Format: Individual

Time: 20 minutes

Materials: Pencils, copies of crossword puzzle on next page

1. Give each student a copy of the puzzle.

2. Make sure everyone understands the directions.

3. Collect and check the puzzles when everyone is done.

Job Stress

Name: _____

Directions: Complete the crossword puzzle below.

Across

5. Overwhelm

6. To get ready for

7. An argument

8. To get in the way

9. Gets you going

10. Disruptive influence

Down

1. Try to reach this

2. First things first

3. To give power to

4. Takes energy away

Job Stress Answer Key

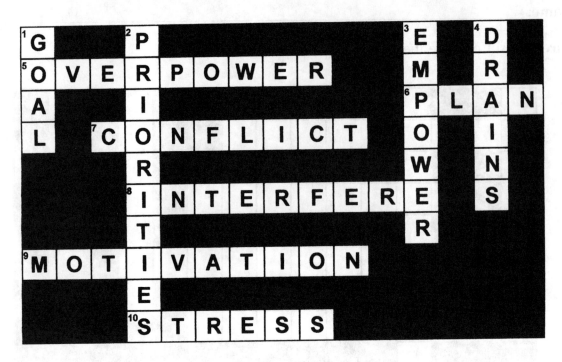

Chapter 12

Objectives

- Understanding that changes in today's world are constant; we must expect the unexpected.

- Seeing how and why the job market has changed.

- Preparing for future trends.

Changing Times and Trends in the Workplace

Rationale for This Topic

This is your SURVIVAL EDGE.

Understanding and preparing for current and oncoming changes is important for job survival.

Many recent changes have made it more difficult to find work.

Education is powerful. Prepare for future trends.

This is stuff you MUST KNOW.

Working Vocabulary

- **Change.** Change is to cause to be different (alter).

- **Multitasking.** Performing more than one task at once.

- **Automation.** Machines doing the work of people.

- **Trend.** A trend is a direction of movement (a course).

- **Downsizing.** When a company shrinks its number of employees.

For Discussion

As I said in Chapter 1, there is one thing that we can always depend on in the working world: Change is constant.

It is often difficult to predict change and changing trends.

We do have signs and can make predictions based on what is happening in the changing world, such as international trade, the Internet, automation, world economy, outsourcing jobs, and integration of multinational cultures.

Changes have affected working people everywhere. We have not been prepared for all of these changes. Many have come about due to unexpected events such as 9/11, the downturn in the economy, and a shrinking labor force.

Ask the students, "Can you name some signs of workplace change?" Write them on the board.

Presentation Suggestions

Use with Pages 179–180

Discuss the vocabulary words. Have students complete the Stop and Think on pages 179–180. Ask several students to share what they were doing on 9/11. Lead into an open discussion how their lives have changed personally and in the world of work.

Remind students of how rapidly change can happen.

Use with Pages 180–182

Have the students read silently pages 181–182 up to "Future Trends." Discuss how multi-tasking, automation, and temporary services have affected the job market.

Use with Pages 182–184

Have a student read "Future Trends" aloud. Discuss what goods producing employment vs. service producing employment means. Have them silently read the following section and complete the Stop and Think. Ask several students to share their answers.

Ask the following questions and list answers on the board:

What are your parents saying about today's job market?

What are your friends saying about today's job market?

Activities

Multitasking

Use: after page 181

Format: groups of 4

Time: 25–30 minutes

Materials: copies of multitasking cards (see next page)

1. Divide class into groups of 4.

2. Explain that this exercise will be about multitasking.

3. Pass out a blank role card to each student.

4. Ask each group to write a job and four tasks that a person performs in that job. Explain that they will be acting these tasks out and the other groups will be guessing what the job is. Encourage them to pick tasks that are easy to act out, such as a waitress bringing food to a table, not an accountant balancing books.

5. Within each group, have them decide who will perform which task.

6. Have each group perform in front of the class, all 4 people doing their assigned task at the same time. No words are to be spoken.

7. Have the other groups guess what the job is.

Role-Play Cards

Job: _____

Tasks: _____

    1. _____

    2. _____

    3. _____

    4. _____

Job: _____

Tasks: _____

    1. _____

    2. _____

    3. _____

    4. _____

Job: _____

Tasks: _____

    1. _____

    2. _____

    3. _____

    4. _____

Job: _____

Tasks: _____

    1. _____

    2. _____

    3. _____

    4. _____

Job: _____

Tasks: _____

    1. _____

    2. _____

    3. _____

    4. _____

Skills

Use: after page 182

Format: whole class

Time: 25–30 minutes

Materials: paper

1. Instruct students to close their workbooks.

2. Divide the class into groups of 4.

3. Explain that in this exercise we will look at various common jobs that you are familiar with.

4. Appoint a secretary for each group to keep a list of answers.

5. Read the following job one at a time:

   Food service in a cafeteria

   Receptionist

   Grocery stores and discount stores

   Janitorial service

6. Have each group list all the skills and duties that are required for that job.

7. When the groups are finished, have each secretary read the answers to the class.

8. Discuss the different skills and duties required for each job.